Time Management:
The Ultimate Time Management Guide

With techniques, tips and tricks for beginners

Table of contents

Introduction

Time is a currency we would all like to maximize. There are only 24 hours in a day. Eight hours (or less) go to sleeping, recharging for the onslaught of tasks that you must face in the morning. Another eight hours go to work, especially if you work regular shifts in an office. That leaves eight hours for you to eat three healthy meals, bathe, brush your teeth, travel back and forth from your house to the office, progress with paperwork or bills, read a book or spend time with your family.

With so much to do every single day, a lot of us often find ourselves wishing for an extra hour or two. Why can't each day have 26 hours instead? A lot of us could use those crucial two hours to catch up on sleep or friends and family - especially after such a long, tiring day at work. It seems unfair and difficult to manage a 24-hour day, doesn't it?

Well, the harsh truth of the matter is this: most of us simply don't know how to maximize time, how to get 26 hours of work and leisure done in a regular 24-hour day. Don't despair. While most of us have no clue when it comes to time management, there are certainly more ways than one to learn all about it. This is what successful people bank on - the truth that anyone learns to manage time efficiently, and squeeze an extra two hours of productivity into the usual 24 hour day.

The fact that you are reading this book means that you are capable of thinking and concluding like those successful people. You have realized that time really is gold, and that if you can't manage your hours effectively, you will always be more than just a little productive every day. The fact that you are reading this book right now means that you are ready to embark on a journey that, though difficult at first, will certainly change your life for the better.

This book was written for people from all walks of life. Whether you are a university student, trying to make the most of your review time before your final exams, or a parent struggling to juggle work, household chores, and raising your kids, this book is definitely right for you. If you are a professional, an employee or a manager, then this book will help you make the most out of your day, and get more work done than you ever thought you could-- without experiencing burnout.

To give you a better idea about what this book can do for you, here are some of the topics you will learn about as you read from chapter to chapter:

1. The Basic Principles of Time Management
2. Secrets and Techniques to Master the Art of Time Management
3. Practical Tips specifically targeted for students, parents, and professionals
4. How to make the most of 2 hours
5. The power of 10 minutes

This book will show you how you can finish all the tasks you have for the day, without losing important time to be with your family or your friends. If you've always wanted to pursue a sport, investment or hobby, but just never found the time to juggle all your responsibilities and make time for yourself, then do not hesitate to learn all you can from this book.

Read on, and let the art and science of time management change your life forever!

Thank you for downloading this book. I hope you enjoy it, and learn a lot from it!

Do you want to receive free bonus content and updates on my other books? Then don't forget to subscribe to my mailing list at:

http://eepurl.com/XzxDL

Chapter 1: The Two Core Principles of Time Management

Before you go into the specifics, secrets and techniques of time management, you must have a few principles with which to start your work. In this chapter, you will be introduced to two core principles that you can master easily.

Managing your time effectively and efficiently are two different things. People who have mastered the art of time management know the difference between being effective and efficient, and have found ways of being both. So what is the difference between being effective and being efficient? How do you incorporate those two important qualities into your time management practice?

Principle 1: Learning to be Effective AND Efficient

Effectiveness focuses on the adequacy of your performance to complete a certain task or solve a specific problem. On the other hand, efficiency is more concerned with wasting as little time and effort as possible to complete a task, while gaining greater or better output.

To give you a better understanding of how these two qualities differ, and what impact they have on your day to day life, here is an example.

Effectiveness vs. Efficiency: A Case Study

John, Matt and Harry are good friends. They own a motorcycle repair shop. They work equal hours every day, and come home with the same amount of wages. However, Harry noticed that he was getting more client requests than both John and Matt. Determined to find out why this was happening, Harry observed the way John and Matt worked, and compared it to his way of getting things done. As Harry watched his friends, he realized that John and Matt had different styles of working on the motorcycles.

John rushed into his work without thoroughly thinking about the motorcycle's problems. He didn't consult any manuals or ask any advice. Though he usually did the right thing, he worked a lot slower than Matt. John was effective at his work because he was able to complete the repairs and client requests correctly. However, John was not efficient because he wasted too much time puttering about the motorcycle, and trying to repair each one by trial and error.

Matt was a faster worker than John. He knew exactly what the problems of the motorcycles were, and how he could fix them quickly. However, Matt also focused on other things before tackling the main problem of the client's motorcycle. He liked to clean the entire body first, then go on to shine the handles, buff the mirrors, and oil the brakes. Matt was efficient at his work because of his capability to get things done quickly and with minimal effort. However, Matt was not effective because he started with tasks that did not concern the main problem of the motorcycle. Yes, the cleaning and shining helped, but it wasn't solving the repair problems the client had asked Matt to work on.

Harry thought about how he worked on the motorcycles that were passed into his charge. He realized that he immediately tackled the main problem of the motorcycle in question, but not before he was absolutely sure of what he was supposed to do. He took a few minutes to consult manuals and choose the right tools. Once he was convinced that his strategy was correct, he worked on the main problem without allowing himself to be distracted by the other things he could do to improve the motorcycle's condition. These small differences in Harry's work style made him both effective and efficient. These small differences also happened to be responsible for Harry's longer client list and better feedback reports.

Applying Efficiency and Effectiveness to Every Day Tasks

Do you see how important it is to be both effective and efficient when it comes to managing your time? The first principle of time management is to learn the difference between being effective and being efficient, and then incorporating both of those qualities into everything you do in your day to day tasks. Whenever you are in the middle of completing tasks, ask yourself these questions designed to show whether or not you are being efficient, effective, or both.

1. Do you know what you are supposed to do?
2. Have you solved problems like this one before?
3. Do you have a quick and reliable source of knowledge to help you get the job done?
4. Are there any distractions around?
5. Have you identified the main problem?
6. Is your strategy time demanding or effort intensive?

When you answer these questions, think of how John, Matt and Harry work, and remember why Harry's style of working and managing his time is both more efficient and effective. Applying Harry's simple work style to yours could save you more minutes than you ever thought it would.

Principle 2: Differentiating between Urgency and Importance

Now that you know what the difference between efficiency and effectiveness is, you should be able to grasp the concepts of urgency and importance with ease. You see, being able to differentiate which of your tasks are urgent or important will help you prioritize and schedule your tasks accordingly. This means that you will have a clearer view of what you need to achieve within a set time, and you will be able to focus on the tasks that matter the most, thereby maximizing a few hours each day.

Urgent tasks are the ones that demand your immediate attention. However, these tasks are not necessarily crucial to your every day schedule. There may be times when your urgent tasks impose big consequences on your work, lifestyle and so on, but generally urgent tasks sit on a lower rank than those tagged under the important tasks.

Important tasks, on the other hand, are tasks that demand your immediate attention and commitment. Failing to respond effectively and efficiently to important tasks will definitely affect your schedule and time limit negatively. These are the tasks that you cannot put on hold unless absolutely necessary.

To give you a better understanding of how to differentiate between urgent and important tasks, read the example below.

Urgency vs. Importance: A Case Study

Sally is stressed at work. She was given more than seven documents to encode by her boss just when she was about to leave the office. Her boss told her that the deadline for the encoded documents is in 24 hours. Sally still has to take her children home, cook dinner, and help her kids with their assignments before putting them to bed. She also has the laundry to fold and the house to clean. Her mother also sent her a few files that need to be edited. With a sigh, she leaves the office and heads straight to her kids' school. Though she wanted to get a head start on the documents, Sally understands that her kids will be worried if she does not show up on time. She knows that the safety and wellbeing of her kids are at the top of her priorities because of its urgency and importance.

At home, Sally whips up some pasta for her children, and then helps them finish their homework. She puts them to bed early, and promises that they will eat in an ice cream parlor on Saturday. Sally then sits at her computer and encodes the documents as fast and as accurately as she can. She decided to put the chores on hold, not because they weren't important, but because they were less urgent than her boss' deadline. She finishes typing the documents, and manages to clean the dishes before going to bed. The next day, her boss, impressed with her hard work and punctuality, kindly gave her a day off. Now, Sally has the entire day to finish the chores she put on hold for her work. Sally also has ample time to edit the files that her mother sent her.

Sally's situation is one that you can see every day. Given extra work, household chores and children to take care of, she had to decide which tasks are urgent or important, and both. The task that was both urgent and important by the time Sally left the office was getting her kids home. Afterward, she had to feed them, help them with their homework, and get them to bed. For Sally, all those little tasks were important. She had to finish them first to avoid the consequences of having her children go hungry or ill prepared for school the next day.

After that, she was finally able to settle down with her boss' documents. This task was also urgent and important, but she designated it to a later time, because she deemed her kids' welfare more important than her work. Lastly, Sally decided that the household chores were urgent, but not really important. She could and would catch up with her chores whenever she had the time. The same goes for the files her mother sent her.

Applying Urgency and Importance to your Every Day Tasks

Whenever you find yourself amidst a number of tasks, remember that the best way to get them all done in time is to decide which of the tasks are urgent and important, and then determine the degree of urgency or importance of the individual tasks. To help you do that, here are a few pointers you can refer to when making your decisions about which tasks to finish first.

1. The first task you must accomplish should be urgent AND important.

2. The next tasks you must accomplish should be more important than urgent.
3. After that, respond to the tasks that are more urgent than important.
4. Lastly, do not let the tasks that are neither important nor urgent distract you from your priorities.
5. Focus on one task at a time, and finish each with the same level of effort and quality.

Chapter 2: Qualities and Goals of an Excellent Time Manager

Becoming an excellent time manager doesn't happen overnight. It happens as you grow with discipline and passion. It happens when you learn to classify your long-term goals from your short-term goals. It happens when you begin to see time as something that is manageable, instead of something chaotic. In this chapter, you will be introduced to the qualities and goals of an excellent time manager.

You will learn how to further apply effectiveness and efficiency, urgency and importance, as the latter segment of this chapter deals a little with goal-setting. By the end of this chapter, you should have a good idea as to what kind of goals and qualities you have, and how you can improve yourself as a time manager.

Qualities of Excellent Time Managers

While there are a number of qualities all time managers must have, the list below covers the three essential traits you must have as you endeavor to make the most of each day. These three qualities are the foundation for every other trait you will pick up along the way, and are crucial to your development as an effective and efficient time manager.

1. Discipline

Oh yes, discipline is the number one quality all excellent time managers share. You see, during the first few days of your journey as a better time manager, you will no doubt be excited. You will be focused, committed to your work. You will stick to your carefully planned schedules and make sure that you keep your eyes on your goals. But after the excitement and hype have gone, you will feel tired, and suddenly, keeping up with the schedule you set for yourself becomes a chore.

Maybe you could sneak an email break here or a Facebook update for just five minutes. Maybe you could tweak your schedule a bit- after all, you were the one who made it in the first place, so doesn't that entitle you to adjusting it so you have twenty minutes of surfing the Internet before working on a major project?

The truth is that this step of the journey, this phase where you are suddenly faced with indecision and the temptation to veer off course for just a little while — this is the phase you must overcome with flying colors. This is the most important challenge you will have to hurdle, and for that you need discipline.

Discipline shapes every other quality that excellent time managers have. Discipline helps you increase your focus and patience, while ensuring that your outputs are all of high quality. Without discipline, you would not be able to become an excellent time manager, much less get over the phase of indecision and temptations.

Still, since you reached this part of the book, it is safe to assume that you are truly interested in taking control of your time, and in making yourself a better person. You have amassed enough discipline and passion, and you will surely go a long way so long as you keep sharpening your skills and qualities such as this.

2. Gracefulness under Pressure

The ability to calmly assert your authority over situations of panic or disorderliness is one that you must be willing to train from the very start of your venture with time management. Even if you have a thoroughly detailed schedule, there will be times when things won't go according to plan. In some situations, you will be able to get everything under control with a few scheduling tweaks, but sometimes, you will be faced with ordeals that seem to go nowhere but downhill.

During trials like these, you must have the ability to act gracefully under pressure. This means that, despite the panic, or the disastrous consequences that may have jeopardized your plans and schedules, you can remain calm, assertive and alert. You will not let stress get the better of you. Instead, you will act decisively, pick things up little by little, and be unafraid to start again.

3. Passion

The last, but equally important essential trait of any excellent time manager is passion. Passion for what, though? For getting more work done than you thought possible? Well yes, that could be a good motivator- but the real passion you must nurture here is the passion to take control of your time, instead of letting time control you. You must have a passion for getting everything done on time, and with more than just average standards. You must have a passion for having enough time for your family and friends, for your hobbies, your interests, and your growth as a person.

In short, you must have the passion to live every single day to its maximum capacity. You must have the passion to seize each hour with zest, and turn each 60 minutes into the best and most productive hour of your life.

Effective Goal-setting for Better Time Management

To set goals effectively, you must use the second core principle of time management—that is to distinguish between the urgent and important tasks. In this segment, you will be introduced to the three main types of goals, as well as tips on how to set better, more realistic goals in the future.

The Three Main Types of Goals

Goal-setting is often a personal task, unless of course, you must plan a schedule with your teammates or colleagues. The three main types of goals will make it easier for you to categorize your tasks, and aid you in creating an efficient schedule.

Short-term Goals

Short-term goals are usually centered on the different activities of our day to day lives. These goals are often basic and part of our routine. They can be done daily or weekly.

Short-term goals are relatively simple and easy compared to medium-term and long-term goals. They demand most of your attention, but will no longer require your time after you have finished them.

An example of short-term goal is the assignment given to students at the end of a school day. Remember when you were a high school student and you had to take home math problems or history reports almost every day? Or what about your literature book reports? Wasn't there a time when you were tasked to read a chapter of a certain book every two or three days? Those are examples of short-term goals.

See, they may demand your immediate and full attention, but once you dedicate a day or two to completing these kinds of goals, you can move on to the other things listed in your schedule. These are the goals that you should never put on hold, as they will only pile up and force you to cram.

Medium-term Goals

Now medium-term goals take longer to complete than short-term goals. The time it takes to complete a medium-term goal can range from two weeks to two months. They take more compounded effort and time to finish, but often have bigger rewards than short-term goals.

> Now, if daily assignments are short-term goals, then the final exams and the grades that come out every semester can be considered examples of medium-term goals.
>
> Medium-term goals are also known for being the stepping stones that lead to the long-term goals. Their success is an indicator of how well a long-term goal will turn out to be.

Long-term Goals

As the name suggests, long-term goals need more than just a few months to be completed. Some long-term goals take several years before they are finished while others take a minimum of a year or two before they are completed.

Long-term goals are reached by accomplishing both short-term and medium-term goals. Think of long-term goals like the homestretch of a horseracing track. They are the last few meters before the finish line. They are what you have completed your short and medium-term goals for. In a sense, long-term goals can be thought of as the great reward after years of hard work.

An example of a long-term goal is to graduate as the class valedictorian, or get a scholarship for a prestigious university. The short-term and medium-term goal examples of daily assignments, exams and yearly grades were all leading to the ultimate goal of being announced top of the graduating class, or receiving a scholarship from your dream university.

Chapter 3 – The Art of Prioritization

Now that you are more adept at telling which tasks are urgent or important, and which goals are for the long, medium or short term, it is time to learn all about prioritization and how you can apply all the concepts discussed so far to create the perfect schedule. In this chapter, you will learn the different ways to prioritize, and how you can make your tasks easier depending on their priority level. This chapter has priority table examples to help guide you and inspire you to make priority tables of your own. By the end of this chapter, you should have the knowledge and the confidence to try organizing your tasks based on the concepts of prioritization.

Prioritize this way, prioritize that way!

There are three main degrees of prioritization. All of them are pretty simple and easy to grasp.

Prioritization according to task deadlines

The first degree or method of prioritization is based mainly on task deadlines. Time constraints are a good motivation for anyone who wants to stay on schedule. If you know that you handle time pressure well, and that you are more motivated to finish your tasks given a specific amount of time, then your prioritization table should focus on the tasks that need to be done as soon as possible, and in the smallest amount of time.

An example of a prioritization table based on time constraints is detailed for you below. This table is modeled around a student's tasks and time limits.

Task	Deadline/Time	Priority

	Limit	
Attend Chess Club Meeting	5:00pm/ 60 minutes	Urgent and Important; Priority #1
Complete Science Homework	8:30pm/ 45 minutes	Urgent and Important; Priority #3
Progress for Mathematics Project	9:30pm/60 minutes	Important; Priority #4
Write Speech for Debate Club	10:30pm/60 minutes	Important; Priority #5
Check Facebook and Twitter accounts	Negotiable	Neither Important nor Urgent; Priority #6
Help mom clear the dishes	8:00pm/ 20 minutes	Urgent; Priority # 2

Notice how the priorities still depend on the deadline and time limit that the student set for himself. Even if his science homework was both urgent and important, he still placed clearing the dishes on a higher priority level since the deadline and time limit for that certain task was closer and could be quickly accomplished. Notice also how the student identified checking Facebook and Twitter as neither important nor urgent, and how he did not specify any time limit or deadline for that certain task. As in the first chapter, learning to tell which of your tasks is urgent, important and both will help you a lot when you begin prioritizing and scheduling your day-to-day activities.

Prioritization according to task difficulty

The second degree or method of prioritization is based on the difficulty of a certain task. Some people prefer tackling the more challenging tasks first, before proceeding to the easy tasks. On the other hand, some people like finishing all the easy tasks first before moving on to the more difficult tasks. There is no right or wrong way when it comes to this kind of prioritization. You must create your priority table based on how you view tasks, and how you prefer to work on them.

Below is a sample priority table based on task difficulty made by a journalist named Mary. She likes attacking the easy tasks first so that the rest of her time can be focused on completing the more difficult ones.

Task	Degree of Difficulty	Deadline	Priority
Proofread Feature Article on *Fashion Trends*	Easy; can be finished in less than an hour	Tuesday, 10:00am	Priority #2
Begin project for Client: *Mr. Brown*	Medium; needs at least two hours of research, two hours for first draft	Saturday, 5:00pm	Priority #3
Work on novel: *Under Two Skies*	Difficult; chapter length is variable, writer's block is a factor	(First draft) Three weeks from today, Monday, 4:00pm	Priority #4
Household chores	Easy but tedious; must finish in less than an hour	Today, 7:30pm	Priority #1

Since Mary prefers finishing the easier tasks before moving on to the more difficult tasks, she ranked the household chores and proofreading as the first two priorities on her table. The third priority needed more time and effort, which she could only give if the other easier tasks were completed. The fourth priority on the other hand, required the most time and effort to finish, and Mary also considered that the task's deadline was farther than any of her other tasks. See how Mary saved the most difficult task for last, when she was free of the other tasks she had to complete, and could dedicate indefinite amounts of time to her main project.

Prioritization according to task value

The third degree of prioritization revolves around a certain task or project's value. This kind of prioritization is often used by managers and businessmen and women. Each task is analyzed for their current value and the income they stand to generate. High income or high value projects take the top levels in the priority table, while low income or low value projects take the lower levels.

Consider the sample priority table Mark, a contractor, created to keep track of his projects, their values, and their priority ranking.

Mark is hired by his clients to build their dream homes, office buildings or public venues. Because he is well-established in his line of work, Mark's team has expanded to accommodate several projects at once. Still, Mark knows he must be clear on which projects to prioritize first.

Project	Value	Deadline	Priority
Mr. and Mrs. Garland's Retirement Home	approximately 2,000,000 $	February 2016	Priority #2
BASICS Pharmaceutical Branch	approximately 3,000,000 $	March 2016	Priority #1
Mr. and Mrs. Alison's Condominium Unit	approximately 1,500,000 $	February 2016	Priority #3

Observe how Mark chose between Mr. and Mrs. Garland's retirement home and Mr. and Mrs. Alison's condominium unit based on the project value. While this may seem unfair to Mr. and Mrs. Alison, the fact of the matter is that higher paying projects usually demand more work and time to complete, thus prioritizing the retirement home over the condominium unit was a sensible decision on Mark's behalf. That also explains why Mark placed the BASICS Pharmaceutical branch on Priority #1.

Chapter 4 – Goal-setting and Effective Scheduling

A lot of people learning how to manage their time better benefit from keeping a well-planned schedule. Their schedules are often detailed, and during the first few days of becoming an excellent time manager, their schedules can often be unrealistic or too cramped for real productivity to ensue. This chapter will help you get started on creating the perfect schedule- one that suits your lifestyle, your hours of work, and realistic goals and priorities for the day. By the end of this chapter, you should be excited enough to start planning your own schedule, and equipped with enough knowledge to create a schedule that is perfect for you.

Be Prepared!

There are a few things you must have before you begin creating your ideal schedule. Here is a helpful list for the bare necessities to help you create that perfect schedule!

1. Planner

Many students and professionals use planners to keep track of their work, deadlines and meetings. Originally, planners were simple, lined notebooks that had the dates and hours of every day, week or month. Today however, many other kinds of planners have hit the market as a response to the enthusiasm of the recent generations in documenting their day to day experiences.

You can choose whatever planner you want so long as it suits your needs. Good planners have enough space for you to write the details or notes of your tasks, a few pages for budgeting, personal information, and a separate full page calendar. As long as your chosen planner has these segments, you will be good to go. Remember that your planner doesn't need to be expensive. So long as it is functional and suits your taste, your planner will serve you for the duration of a year.

2. Pen

Some people have a special pen they use for writing only in their planners. Other people like having a multitude of colorful pens they can choose from, so that they can also doodle or scribble on their planners as an alternative to written reminders and prompts.

Whether or not you like old fashioned black ball point pens or trendy green and purple pens doesn't matter. What matters is that you have something to write your schedule and plans with. Like the planner, your pen need not be expensive. You can even reuse old pens that have been left in your office drawer or bag pockets.

3. Desk Calendar

If you don't like using planners, you can always purchase a desk calendar. Get the flat type that you can place on your desk, and immediately note down important meetings or urgent tasks. If you want to add more color to your calendar, then use small Post-it notes or strips of colored paper to help you organize your schedule.

Desk calendars are easy to use in that you can immediately see a whole month in front of you. This transparency will make it easier for you to schedule or reschedule whatever tasks you might have for the current month. You can also flip to the following months and plan ahead.

4. Smart Phone Planner Apps

If you're the kind of person who likes having all the important things in one place, then you can always download planner apps for your smart phone or iPhone. Though different apps offer different features, they basically function in the same way. They help you keep track of your schedule, and can alert you for meetings, dates, or deadlines. Some planner apps also take note of the birthdays of your family and friends, and make sure that you are reminded of them every year.

Aside from being handy, these planner apps are usually free, and are automatically synchronized with your phone data.

5. Laptop and Personal Computer Programs

If there are planner and scheduling applications for smart phones, then there are planner and scheduling programs for laptops and personal computers. If your laptop has a Microsoft Office Suite installed, then you can use the popular MS Outlook as your computer planner.

Like the apps for smart phones, you can also surf the web for free planner and scheduling programs for your laptop or personal computer. They are also usually free, and can even synchronize with your Facebook, Twitter, and email accounts. Though they may not be as handy as smart phone planner apps, they are just as functional and easy to use, and sometimes come with more features designed to suit your personality and taste.

Working on a schedule

Once you have the right materials coupled with the right attitude, you can begin working on your perfect schedule right away. Sit in a quiet place with minimal to no distractions. If you can help it, switch your phone to silent, and disconnect your computer from the Internet. This way, you will be able to focus better on your schedule, and you will finish this task quicker, too.

Step 1: Begin by thinking of all the things you need to do for the day. Take a piece of scratch paper and list down everything you need to remember, track or complete. Do not stop until you are sure you have nothing more to add to your list.

Step 2: Next, take a look of all the tasks you have written. What kind of goals do you see? Are there any long-term or medium-term goals? Or did you only take note of your short-term goals?

If you only wrote a list of short-term goals, try adding a couple of medium and long-term goals as well. It is important that your short-term and medium-term goals act as stepping stones towards the long-term goals.

Ask yourself what you want to achieve a year from now, five years from now, ten years from now. Consider what you must do in order to achieve those long term goals, and write them down.

Step 3: Group all the tasks and goals you have written into short-term, medium-term and long-term categories. It would help if you placed them in a table, so that you can immediately see which goals belong to which group.

Step 4: Work on the short-term goals first. Set deadlines for each task. Depending on the time constraints, difficulty or value, rank each task or goal according to priority. Remember to consider the urgency and importance of each task.

Step 5: By now, you will have a better idea of how your everyday tasks should be accomplished, and how much time you have to finish them. Read through your priorities, tasks and short-term goals again. If you are satisfied, transcribe them into your planner.

Medium-term and Long-term goals

Your medium and long-term goals need not be inscribed in your planner just yet, though you can certainly do so if you prefer it that way. You can take note of your medium and long-term goals in your planner, or you can keep them tacked on one of the walls of your office or home. Whatever you choose, make sure your list of medium and long-term goals are where you can always see them.

The point of knowing and exposing your medium and long-term goals is to motivate you and remind you of how each of your short-term tasks and goals will eventually lead to that six digit savings account, that brand new car or that vacation home in France. Aside from that, your medium and long-term goals will also remind you of how important time management is when it comes to achieving all that you have ever dreamed of.

A few tips for goal-setting and schedule planning

1. **Be realistic.**

As much as you want to finish the laundry, clean the house, cook a magnificent dinner, track and study the market's movement, encode documents for work, manage your finances, draft that new interior design project, watch your favorite soap opera and read to your youngest child—you only have a few hours after you come from home work. You still have to sleep and eat well to have enough strength for the following day, so be realistic. Do not set yourself up for disappointment by setting too many goals, or crowding your schedule with too many tasks.

Instead, reflect upon what you can really achieve within the limited time you have between work and sleep. Set a few achievable goals for the day, and spread your tasks evenly throughout the week.

2. **Set aside time for emergency situations.**

Allot at least thirty minutes for emergency situations. If someone important suddenly calls you with an interesting proposal but your schedule is booked to the last minute, then you might miss a life changing opportunity.

In case those thirty minutes aren't used for emergency situations, then add them to the task that you think needs more of your attention. The point is that you are ready, should something unexpected happen during the day.

3. Set aside time for rest and relaxation.

Do yourself, your schedule and your loved ones a favor. Take care of yourself by making sure that you have enough time to rest every day. Yes, you can have six to eight hours of sleep, but try to include ten minute breaks in-between difficult tasks, or chores that really put you under a lot of stress. While sticking to your schedule is important for you to be an excellent time manager, you must also remember to give time for yourself. Besides, that ten-minute break might be exactly what your new project needs.

Chapter 5 – Time Management Tips for Students

Whether you are a college or high school student, knowing how to maximize your time without getting burned out from stress is crucial to your success in the future. The better you become at time management, the better you become at handling all your homework, projects and social life.

1. Learn how to take down notes properly.

Most students waste several minutes trying to keep up with every word that comes from their teachers. Because they insist on writing down every single word of the lecture, they often find themselves scrambling for more time to jot their notes, or that they are taken by surprise when the teacher calls for a pop quiz. Even if they might have taken 90% of the teacher's lecture, they were so focused on completing their notes that they did not really understand the lesson.

This is why it is important to learn how to take down notes properly. Just like time management and prioritization, you must learn to distinguish which points of the lecture are important. Those are the points you take note of—not word per word, but in your own words, through your own understanding. This way, aside from keeping enough notes for review material, you also train your mind to understand and learn the lesson while the teacher is talking.

Just by learning which points to write down in your notebook, you already save more than just a couple of minutes, as well as reduce the stress that comes from wanting to catch every word of the lesson.

2. Review your notes or reading material every night.

Don't let yourself get used to cramming a whole semester's worth of topics into just a few nights of studying before the final exams. Instead, allot an hour or two to read your notes, research on the things you did not fully comprehend, and do a bit of advanced reading for the next topic. This ensures that you are always ready for pop quizzes or graded recitations. It also saves you long hours of studying the night before the exams or presentation. By making a habit out of reading your notes, you allow your mind to soak information at a steady, reliable pace, instead of forcing yourself to understand all your lessons in just a couple of hours.

3. Reward yourself.

After each study session, allow yourself to watch an episode of your favorite television series. If you made a lot of progress on your thesis or science project, then pig out with your friends while watching a movie before going to sleep.

Remember that you owe it to yourself to have a good time after putting in a decent amount of hours for afterschool work. If you have too many tasks to finish every night, then give yourself the entire Sunday off to do whatever you want. Go to the mall, or camp out in your backyard- just make sure you include time to have fun in your schedule.

4. Learn to say "No."

One of the most common reasons why students fail to submit their homework or projects in time, or ace that critical exam, is because they did not say "No" to distractions. What are these distractions?

Well, some of these distractions come in the form of late-night road trips or parties with friends, but most of the time, distractions come in the form of spending too much time on social networking sites and the Internet. Yes, it is absolutely fine to have fun, but remember that chapter on prioritization and how you should know which tasks to finish first? Well, this is the application of that chapter.

If you do not learn to say "No" to the distractions that prevent you from studying well, then you will never be good at managing your time. Remember that you can always go to a party after your exams, or take a road-trip to somewhere better after you finish your project. Remember that sometimes, sacrifices are necessary if you want to have success.

5. Learn to say "Yes."

On the other hand, there are also some students who are too caught up in studying for finals that they miss out on great opportunities like their school dance, sports competitions, and other such activities. Think of these activities as yet another way to reach your medium and long-term goals of success.

Inasmuch as you need to learn to say "No" to distractions, you also need to learn to say "Yes" to opportunities that will help you grow as a person. Allot time in your schedule to do something educational other than holing up in your room, poring over your textbooks. Keep in mind that a well-rounded person knows how to balance academics and extra-curricular activities, and that such a person is bound to learn and excel more at time management, than those who insist on being a one-trick magician.

Chapter 6 – Time Management Tips for Parents

Parents have the most challenging job of all—to raise respectful, intelligent and confident children. They also happen to have the most chores and side-careers than anyone else in the world. Aside from doing well in their chosen careers, many working parents must also find the time to go to their son's football game, their daughter's ballet recital, schedule family trips, attend parent-teacher conferences, and keep the house clean, the table full of healthy foods, and the children at peace with their siblings.

The work load isn't any lighter for stay-at-home moms and dads either. In fact, looking after the kids every single day can be more tiring than stepping inside an office to work for the regular eight hours. Here are a few tips to help parents, working or stay-at-home, manage their time better.

1. **Mom, Dad, the kids can help.**

Ask the kids to help with the household chores, especially those aged 10 and above. Even the little ones can help out by putting their toys away, or fixing the sofa pillows. Everyone in the family must have a list of chores to do so that mom and dad aren't always puttering around the house. Aside from teaching your kids initiative and responsibility, this will also show them how families work to help each other.

Time-wise, parents will be able to save more minutes than they thought possible when relieved of the simpler house chores. This frees up their time to concentrate on more difficult tasks, or get their much deserved rest.

2. **Keep everything in its proper place.**

A lot of time is wasted by just trying to find where the keys were placed, or where the baby's bottles were last seen. Save crucial minutes by placing toy baskets in the kids' rooms, or by making sure all family members know where to place the keys, the remote, the books and so on.

3. Make the most out of the Internet.

Do you need to pay your bills but can't leave the house without a babysitter? Or maybe you need to shop for groceries but have to pick up your kids from soccer practice? During these situations, the best time-saving solution would be to use the Internet. Nowadays, business transactions, bills payment, and yes, even grocery shopping and delivery can be done over a reliable Internet connection. Make use of your computer and Internet connection to get some chores done with a few clicks of the mouse.

4. Keep the calendar or planner where everyone can see it.

Hang a chore board in the kitchen, or a daily schedule planner in the living room. This will help not only you, but every family member remember their tasks and manage their time a lot better. Plus, it's great fun to cross out or erase finished tasks from the board with your family cheering you on.

5. Think two steps ahead.

Just like chess masters, parents who want to make the most of their time must learn how to think ahead, in order to eliminate repetitive tasks, or chores that take up too much time. Expecting a hectic morning? Cook enough food at dinner so that the leftovers go straight to the microwave and onto the plates at breakfast. Think you'll have a long day at the office? Post chores for your partner and the kids to finish when they get home, and keep standby food in easy to find containers. By thinking about which tasks you can eliminate from your schedule beforehand, you'll save a lot of minutes and effort, plus cut down on the stress.

Chapter 7 – Time Management Tips for Professionals

Professionals, just like students and parents, know the impact that time management skills can have on their social life and career. They are often under the stress of team or managerial projects, critical assignments, and emergency meetings. However, even if they know about the basics of time management, it still takes the same amount of discipline and commitment to actually avoid distractions or excuses to let the work pile up, and then stress about it as they cram efforts, and compromise work quality. The five tips below will help any professional, regardless of what occupation or level, manage his or her time better.

1. **Dedicate at least twenty minutes every day, to plan and keep track of your daily goals and tasks.**

   If you have a clear vision of what you are supposed to accomplish for the day, then there is a higher chance that you will actually finish every task you've set for yourself. You see, knowing about what you have to do, and taking a few minutes to focus your energy on your tasks sometimes make all the difference in a hectic, stressful workday.

2. **Don't skip lunch.**

   Don't skip breakfast either, or dinner. Eat well to function well. Eat healthy meals during break time to replenish the energy you spent in the accounting office or the operations research room. Eat well because if you don't, chances are that you'll find yourself dozing off, or unable to focus on your work. Those few minutes spent taking naps and allowing your mind to wander often add up to an hour or two, if you think about it. You'll also be doing your work much slower, so that's a minus in efficiency. The bottom line is, eat when it's time to eat, because your brain can only function as well as your stomach.

3. **Don't be afraid to hang a "Do Not Disturb" sign on your office door if you really need to finish a difficult task in a few hours.**

Just like students need to learn to say "No" so professionals need to make others in the office understand when it is okay to come in for a casual chat, and when it is not okay to bring in distractions. Keeping your office to yourself for a few hours can boost your productivity so much, you'll probably want to do it more often, especially if your tasks are time-consuming and tiring to finish.

4. **Organize, organize, and organize!**

Clear your desk. Separate scratch paper from important documents. Keep track of your schedule, meetings and deadlines. Keep your coffee mug away from official contracts, and avoid using the last drawer of your desk as a trash can. Clear your space so you can also clear your mind. Unless you are one of those people who work extremely well in messy rooms, pick up after yourself, and keep your place clean. This will save you tons of minutes of paper riffling, key searching, and emergency file organization and so on.

Keep accurate tabs of everything you have in your office. Allot folders or file holders for similar projects, and keep the trash where it should be. Buy a cheap pen holder and other desk organizers to help keep everything you need to work in sight, without overcrowding your workspace.

5. **Learn to walk away when you can't think of anything else. And then come back when you're ready—or when your other tasks are done.**

If you're having a bad day, or your creative juices aren't cooperating with you, and you've been looking at a blank paper for more than an hour, then you must learn to walk away from it. Walk away because you'll be wasting more time if you force yourself to think of something. Walk away because there are other tasks that need your attention, and getting them done early will free up time for you to come back to that impossible project proposal or not-so-catchy pitch. Walk away because sometimes, that's exactly what you need to take control of your time and your stress level.

Chapter 8 – Ten Magic Minutes

What can you do with ten minutes? Refocus your energy, stretch and exercise, eat a healthy snack, plan out your evening or afternoon, and so much more. In this chapter, you will learn more about how ten well-spent minutes can make all the difference in your day. You will also learn how to tell whether your ten minute segments are used to be more productive, or are taken away by distractions and other unnecessary activities. By the end of this chapter, you should have enough ideas with what you can do in ten minutes, and be motivated to make that short span of time really count.

1. **Advance to the next task.**

This is the most common thing people do when they are able to finish work ten minutes earlier than expected. They often add those ten minutes to the next task, find that they finish even earlier, and have fifteen or twenty minutes of free time on their hands. If you're feeling energetic, and you don't want to ruin your work momentum, then just plow through that to-do list of yours, and get through your tasks quicker than your schedule says you should. After you finish with your work, you will not only feel confident and fulfilled, you will also have about half an hour or more to do whatever you want before the next onslaught of chores and tasks come along.

2. **Read a book.**

Grab whatever book is sitting on your shelf, and pick up where you left off. If the book you chose is an anthology, flip to a random page, and read whatever story or poem is on it. Reading broadens the imagination, and helps us learn new things. We are given the chance to meet new people, go to foreign places, and take part in different experiences whenever we open a book.

3. **Write in your journal.**

If you don't feel like reading, maybe writing about your day, or jotting down your thoughts will help you loosen up and get ready for your next task. Writing about anything at all is challenging inasmuch as it offers therapeutic benefits. What's another plus of writing in your journal? Well, if you ever become a famous personality, your journal could be the ticket to a bestselling autobiography that your fans will line up for—or maybe you'll simply enjoy looking back on your life through old, dog-eared journal pages.

4. Doodle and scribble.

If you just need a quick way to release your stress, why not grab a piece of paper, some pens or even some crayons and draw out your fatigue with different colors. Just like writing in your journal, creating doodles and scribbles helps you manage your stress, reenergize and can sometimes give you the creative push you need to make that important project stand out.

5. Listen to music.

Music is the language of the soul. So when you think you're feeling down or too tired to continue with your schedule, plug in your earphones and let your favorite songs blast all your stress away. You can even sing along if you want.

6. Stretch those tired muscles.

Get up from your chair, walk out of your office or house, and stretch both your arms and legs while you're at it. Take a quick walk to and from the coffee shop or the sandwich stall, just to get your blood flow properly, and the oxygen levels in your body to normalize.

7. Have a snack.

Get out the sandwich your partner prepared especially for you, and have a good time eating it all. Or, better yet, share the sandwich with an equally hungry colleague, and take ten minutes to catch up with him or her. Not only will you have shared a satisfying meal, you will also have shared a great, quick conversation.

Now, notice that this list did not contain "Check your email" or "Look at your Facebook notifications" or "Take a nap." Checking your email and Facebook notifications are hardly productive (unless you receive important and urgent emails are regularly). In fact, sitting in front of a computer connected to the Internet can distract you from managing your time well, and can tempt you to extend that ten minute period into half an hour or so.

Save the social networking sites for later, when you are done with everything important. Also, taking a ten minute nap can be troublesome. Instead of reenergizing you, ten minute naps will most probably make you feel even sleepier, or have you wake up with a headache. Save the naps for when you have at least twenty or thirty minutes to spare.

Chapter 9 – An Extra Two Hours!

Haven't you sometimes wished you could have an extra two hours every day to get everything done? Well, this chapter will teach you the secret to getting 26 hours out of the usual 24 hour day.

Understand this first: The truth is, those extra two hours you're asking for has already been given to you. The problem is that you aren't managing your time well enough for you to realize that all your distractions and unnecessary tasks take up that precious two hours, sometimes even three hours or more. You have to understand that the 24 hours in a day are more than enough to get all your work done if you just refrain from doing anything outside of your schedule or anything that has nothing to do with your priorities and goals. Below is a list of tips to help you get back those two hours every day.

1. **Disconnect.**

   Turn off the Internet, or work in a place where there is no Wi-Fi especially if you really need to focus on a particular task and you know that you are easily distracted by Facebook or Twitter. Think about this, how many times do you check your social networking sites? Let's say that in an hour, you casually browse through your social accounts at least three times. During those brief interludes with Facebook, Tumblr, Instagram and so on, you spend an average of five minutes. Five minutes turns to fifteen minutes if you check your accounts regularly. That means your one hour of work was actually just 45 minutes of work and 15 minutes of distractions.

   If the Internet is inescapable or vital to your line of work, then look for programs or applications that ban social networking sites and other irrelevant websites for the duration of your working hours. Some of these applications are free and can be customized to, for example, ban you from accessing Facebook for the next two hours.

This way, you can only use the Internet for relevant searches, and your one hour of work doesn't get spoiled by 15 minutes of online distractions.

2. Capture those precious two hours.

What time of the day are you usually most productive? Are you a morning or night person? Do you work better in the wee hours, or the late afternoon? Figure out what time you can work without feeling tired, and capture those hours. Make it a habit to turn those two hours into a productive time. Depending on what time you work best, and how dedicated you are to your tasks, you can complete jobs that usually take up three or more hours in those two precious hours or less.

3. After a dedicated two hour phase with work or chores, it's time to loosen up.

Avoid feeling burned out by your tasks. Remember those ten minute magic tricks to help you feel more energized and creative? Pick one of them, and allow yourself to release stress and pent up energy. You deserve a good ice breaker after being focused on a chore for two hours, after all.

4. Recheck your schedule for too much free time.

Look at the schedule you created. How much time goes to resting or playing around? Did you allot more than an hour? Well then, there's the answer to your missing two hours of the day. While it is necessary and important to include quality rest and recreation in your schedule, overdoing it may in fact, be counterproductive. So recheck your schedule and cross out the unnecessary, the whimsical, and the silly. Add them up, and you'll realize where those two extra hours have gone.

5. Go back to the basics.

Clear your desk. Focus on the task at hand. Stick to your schedule. Stay disciplined.

At the end of the day, your choices will define just how many productive hours you spent, and how many hours you wasted. Sometimes the best way to get that extra two hours is to go back to the basics. Check your priorities and sort them out. Are you still as disciplined and committed to managing your time as when you started? Are you still willing to make a few sacrifices whenever necessary to reach your medium and long-term goals?

Keep time management as simple as this: Work when it's time to work, without distractions and without excuses. You'll soon understand why you don't need to ask for an extra two hours every day. Twenty four hours is more than enough, if you manage your time wisely.

Conclusion

I hope this book was able to help you to show you how to be an excellent time manager through commitment, creativity and discipline.

The next step is to apply all that you have learned from this book, and actively seek self-improvement in terms of managing your time better.

Remember that time is as precious as gold, if not even more so. Therefore, it is your responsibility to make the most out of every day, every week, month and year, until all your goals have been achieved. Do not be discouraged if you find yourself struggling to commit to your priorities and schedule. Becoming an excellent time manager takes time and a lot of dedication. Go through the process slowly, and hold on to the vital lessons you learn along the way.

Keep in mind that the best time manager isn't the one who manages to finish a hundred tasks in eight hours, but the one who knows how to balance his or her time between work, leisure, family, and health.

Finally, if you enjoyed this book, please take the time to share your thoughts and post a review on Amazon. It'd be greatly appreciated! Thank you and good luck!

For more **free** bonus content and updates you can subscribe to my mailing list below:
http://eepurl.com/XzxDL

Check out my other books:

Binary options University:
http://www.amazon.com/Binary-Options-University-profitable-strategies-ebook/dp/B00HCDGZ6Q

Forex for beginners:
http://www.amazon.com/Forex-beginners-trading-analysis-investment-ebook/dp/B00HZ34H54/